toast it!

toast it!

bruschetta • brioche • crostini • ciabatta • focaccia

This edition published 2011
LOVE FOOD is an imprint of Parragon Books Ltd

Parragon
Queen Street House
4 Queen Street
Bath BA1 1HE, UK

ISBN: 978-1-4454-2806-2
Printed in China

Internal design by Talking Design
Photography by Bob Wheeler
Home economy by Valerie Barrett and Sandra Baddeley
Additional recipes and text by Bridget Jones

Notes for the Reader

This book uses both metric and imperial measurements. Follow the same units of
measurement throughout; do not mix metric and imperial. All spoon measurements are level:
teaspoons are assumed to be 5 ml, and tablespoons are assumed to be 15 ml. Unless otherwise
stated, milk is assumed to be full fat, eggs and individual vegetables are medium, and pepper
is freshly ground black pepper.

The times given are an approximate guide only. Preparation times differ according to the
techniques used by different people and the cooking times may also vary from those given.
Optional ingredients, variations or serving suggestions have not been included in the
calculations.

Recipes using raw or very lightly cooked eggs should be avoided by infants, the elderly,
pregnant women, convalescents and anyone suffering from an illness. Pregnant and
breastfeeding women are advised to avoid eating peanuts and peanut products. Sufferers
from nut allergies should be aware that some of the ready-made ingredients used in the
recipes in this book may contain nuts. Always check the packaging before use.

Contents

Introduction

Toasting to perfection – that is, getting the right thickness, temperature and texture – is easy with a little attention to ingredients and technique. Adding toppings or fillings, experimenting with different breads and toasting for all occasions is about fun cooking and fabulous eating!

Breads

Traditional fine, close-textured bread toasts evenly, and becomes crisp outside and soft inside without collapsing or becoming sticky inside when hot. Toasted slowly, thin sliced bread becomes very crisp.

Wholemeal, granary, rye and mixed-grain breads make delicious, nutty toast. Walnut and seeded breads are good for topping or filling. Semi-sweet fruit breads are excellent simply buttered, with sweet spreads, or topped with fruit and grilled.

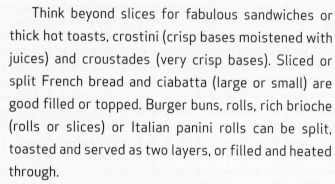

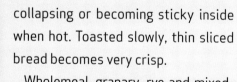

Think beyond slices for fabulous sandwiches or thick hot toasts, crostini (crisp bases moistened with juices) and croustades (very crisp bases). Sliced or split French bread and ciabatta (large or small) are good filled or topped. Burger buns, rolls, rich brioche (rolls or slices) or Italian panini rolls can be split, toasted and served as two layers, or filled and heated through.

Try croissants, crumpets, muffins or waffles for different shapes and textures. Top focaccia, flat breads, Indian naan or Greek pitta; toast tortilla wraps plain or filled. The variations are simply endless, but this collection gives some great ideas for getting started.

Spreads and Fats

Good butter is the only topper for plain toast. It is best to use lightly salted or salted butter, but unsalted low-fat spreads and reduced-fat butters make toast soggy, so these are best avoided if possible. Olive oil is delicious for savoury toasts – brush it lightly on the top side of the bread before toasting. Fat forms a barrier under moist toppings to prevent toast going soft, but there's no need for fat under toasted cheese.

Equipment

• **Grill** Versatile for toasting all sorts of breads, toppings and fillings, or heating layers. Vary temperature settings and distance from the heat source to control cooking. Place food on a rack in a grill pan for fat to drip away and to keep the underside crisp; cook on foil to catch juices or toppings that run.

• **Griddle** A ridged griddle can be used on the hob or (with suitable handles) under the grill. This gives characteristic stripes at high heat or the food gradually toasts evenly if the griddle is not fiercely hot. Under the grill, a griddle will cook the underside as the top toasts.

• **Sandwich toaster or contact grill** Two hot plates that cook sandwiches easily. Light fillings that cook quickly from raw go on the hottest setting; reduce the heat for heavier fillings. Some have cups for deep-filled sandwiches or plates that rest slightly apart for cooking toppings.

• **Pop-up toaster** Variable settings are essential for evenly toasting breads of different thickness or from frozen. Many take different types of bread, including muffins, crumpets or croissants. Special non-stick cooking bags can be used for sandwiches.

• **Toasting fork** Traditional and now funky and fashionable for barbecues or an open fire. Large or small expanding forks are great for marshmallows, chunks of bread, muffins or crumpets.

Breakfast
Bites

Perfect Toast

makes 1 slice

Preheat the grill to a medium–high setting and warm a plate. Place the bread on a rack in the grill pan and toast for about 2 minutes on each side, until evenly golden and crisp. Turn once.

Take the pan from under the grill but leave the toast on the rack. Have the butter ready and spread it on top of the freshly toasted surface. Immediately transfer the toast to the warmed plate, cut it in half with a serrated knife and enjoy plain or with spreads.

ingredients

1 slice traditional white bread, 1.5 cm/$3/4$ inches thick

about 1 tbsp butter, softened

Hot Smoked Salmon, Tomato &
Cream Cheese Bagel

serves 2

Preheat the grill to a medium–high setting. Slice the bagels in half horizontally and place them cut sides down on the rack in the grill pan. Toast until browned, then turn over.

Cover the bottom halves of the bagels with tomato slices. Sprinkle with lemon zest and spring onion, then season with pepper (but not salt – the smoked salmon will be salty when grilled). Trickle a hint of olive oil over the tomatoes. Grill for 1–2 minutes, until the bagels are toasted and the tomatoes are lightly cooked. Remove the top halves and set aside.

Arrange the smoked salmon slices on the tomatoes, wrinkling them slightly, and replace them under the grill for a minute, to lightly cook the salmon and brown the edges in places.

Top each with a couple of dollops of cream cheese and the bagel lids. Serve at once with lemon wedges for adding a squeeze of juice.

ingredients

2 bagels

2 tomatoes, thinly sliced

grated zest of 1 lemon

1 spring onion, chopped

pepper

olive oil

4 slices smoked salmon (about 125 g/$4^1/2$ oz)

4 tbsp cream cheese

lemon wedges, to serve

Toasted Cheese
Sandwich with Egg

serves 1

Preheat the grill to a medium–high setting. Prepare a small pan of simmering water or an egg poacher.

Toast the bread lightly on both sides on the rack in the grill pan. Top one of the slices of bread with ham. Trim off any large areas of overlapping ham and place them on top. Overlap the tomatoes on the ham and sprinkle with the snipped chives and parsley sprigs. Top with the cheese slices. Season with pepper (there will probably be enough salt in the ham) and drizzle with a little olive oil, then cover with the second slice of bread.

Toast the sandwich on both sides until crisp and golden. Meanwhile, break the egg into a cup. Swirl the simmering water and drop the egg into the middle of the swirl, then poach it for about 3 minutes, until the white is set and the yolk still soft. (Cook the egg for a shorter or longer time, to taste.) Alternatively, cook the egg in a poaching pan with cups. Use a slotted spoon to lift the egg from the pan, draining it thoroughly.

Serve the sandwich on a warmed plate, topped with the poached egg. Top with a little butter, if liked, so that it melts over the egg. Serve immediately.

ingredients

2 slices good white or wholemeal bread

1 thick slice cooked ham

1 large tomato, thinly sliced

about 1 tbsp snipped fresh chives

small bunch of fresh flat-leaf parsley, stalks discarded

2 slices mild cheese, such as Monterey, Wensleydale, Cheshire or mild cheddar

pepper

olive oil

1 egg

small knob of soft butter (optional)

Toasted English Muffins with
Blueberries & Bacon

serves 2

Preheat the grill to a medium–high setting. Slice the muffins horizontally into two layers and place them, cut sides down, on the rack in the grill pan.

Lay the bacon rashers on the rack and cook until the tops of the muffins are toasted and the bacon is lightly cooked on one side.

Turn the muffins and divide the blueberries between the bottom halves. Invert the bacon on to the blueberries, covering them completely. Cook for a further 2 minutes, removing the top halves as soon as they are toasted and the bottom when the bacon is browned and crisp.

Place the muffin bases on warmed plates, drizzle with maple syrup, if liked, and add the muffin tops. Serve at once.

ingredients

2 English muffins

2 lean bacon rashers

100 g/4 oz blueberries

2 tsp maple syrup (optional)

Ham & Cheese
Croissant

serves 1

Preheat the grill to a medium–high setting. Slice the croissant horizontally in half, then lay it, cut sides up, on the rack in the grill pan.

Top each croissant half with a slice of cooked ham, overlapping the halves, and spread with a little mustard, if liked. Then top with the cheese, cutting and overlapping the cheese slices to fit the croissant. Grill for about 2 minutes, until the cheese has melted. The croissant will be warmed through and beginning to brown around the edges.

If including the egg, overlap the slices on the bottom layer. Use a knife to scoop any melted cheese off the foil and on to the croissant, then invert the top in place. Serve at once.

ingredients

1 croissant

2 thin slices cooked ham, halved

mustard (optional)

2 slices hard cheese, such as Cheddar, Gruyère or Emmental (about 25 g/1 oz)

1 egg, hard-boiled and sliced (optional)

French Toast
with Maple Syrup

serves 4–6

Preheat the oven to 140°C/275°F/Gas Mark 1. Break the eggs into a large, shallow bowl and beat together with the milk, cinnamon and salt to taste. Add the bread slices and press them down so that they are covered on both sides with the egg mixture. Leave the bread to stand for 1–2 minutes to soak up the egg mixture, turning the slices over once.

Melt half the butter with $1/2$ tablespoon of oil in a large frying pan. Add as many bread slices to the pan as will fit in a single layer and cook for 2–3 minutes until golden brown.

Turn the bread slices over and cook until golden brown on the other side. Transfer the French toast to a plate and keep warm in the oven while cooking the remaining bread slices, adding extra oil to the pan if necessary.

Serve the French toast with the remaining butter melting on top and warm maple syrup for pouring over.

ingredients

6 eggs

175 ml/6 fl oz milk

$1/4$ tsp ground cinnamon

12 slices day-old challah or plain white bread

about 4 tbsp butter or margarine, plus extra to serve

$1/2$ –1 tbsp sunflower or corn oil

salt

warm maple syrup, to serve

Toasted English Muffins with Honey-glazed Bacon & Eggs

serves 2

Preheat the grill to a medium–high setting. Slice the muffins horizontally in half, then lay them cut sides up on the rack in the grill pan. Grill until lightly browned, then turn and cook on the other side. Reserve and keep warm.

Preheat the oven to 140°C/275°F/Gas Mark 1. Heat a non-stick frying pan over a medium heat. Lay the bacon rashers in the pan and cook until lightly browned, then turn and cook the other side.

Warm the honey slightly and brush each rasher lightly with it. Cook the bacon for a further 1 minute or until it takes on a slight glaze. Remove from the pan and keep warm in the preheated oven. Mix the sweetcorn and the tomatoes together and then poach the eggs in a poaching pan with cups.

Butter the warm muffins and add the honey-glazed bacon and eggs, topped with a spoonful of the sweetcorn and tomato mixture.

ingredients

2 English muffins

6 rindless unsmoked bacon rashers

1 tbsp clear honey

85 g/3 oz canned sweetcorn kernels, drained

2 small tomatoes, diced

4 eggs

1 tbsp chopped fresh parsley

salt and pepper

butter

Croque Monsieur

serves 2

Spread half the cheese on 2 slices of bread and top each with a slice of ham and the remaining bread.

For the white sauce, melt the butter with the oil in a small heavy-based saucepan over a medium heat. Add the flour and stir for 1 minute. Take the pan off the heat and pour in the milk, stirring constantly. Return the pan to the heat and continue stirring for one minute or until the sauce is smooth and thickened. Remove the pan from the heat and stir in the remaining cheese and pepper. Set aside and keep warm.

Beat the egg in a bowl. Add 1 sandwich and press down to coat on both sides, then remove from the bowl and repeat with the other sandwich. Preheat the grill to high. Line a baking tray with foil and set aside. Melt the butter for frying in a frying pan over a medium–high heat and fry the sandwiches until golden brown on both sides.

Transfer the sandwiches to the baking tray and spread the white sauce over the top. Place under the grill, about 10 cm/4 inches from the heat, and grill for 4 minutes until golden and brown.

ingredients

100 g/3^1/$_2$ oz Gruyère or Emmenthal cheese, grated

4 slices white bread, with the crusts trimmed

2 thick slices ham

1 small egg, beaten

40 g/1^1/$_2$ oz unsalted butter, for frying

for the white sauce

30 g/1 oz unsalted butter

1 tsp sunflower oil

^{1}/$_2$ tbsp plain flour

125 ml/4 fl oz warm milk

pepper

Chive Scrambled
Eggs with Brioche

serves 2

Break the eggs into a medium bowl and whisk gently with the cream. Season to taste with salt and pepper and add the snipped chives.

Melt the butter in a sauté pan and pour in the egg mixture. Leave to set slightly, then move the mixture towards the centre of the pan using a wooden spoon as the eggs begin to cook. Continue in this way until the eggs are cooked but still creamy.

Lightly toast the brioche slices in a toaster or under the grill and place in the centre of two warmed plates. Spoon over the scrambled eggs and serve immediately, garnished with whole chives.

ingredients

4 eggs

100 ml/$3^1/_2$ fl oz single cream

salt and pepper

2 tbsp snipped fresh chives, plus

4 whole fresh chives to garnish

25 g/1 oz butter

4 slices brioche loaf

Time
for Brunch

Minted Summer
Brie on Pitta

serves 2

Cut the brie into two equal wedges, then slice them horizontally into two layers and replace in the freezer to keep the cheese very firm, but not frozen. Reserve a couple of mint sprigs for garnish, then discard the stalks from the others and shred the leaves.

Preheat the grill to a medium–high setting. Toast the pitta breads on one side, then place them, untoasted sides up, onto a piece of cooking foil on the rack in the grill pan.

Cover the pitta with the cucumber, taking the slices right over the edge, and sprinkle with the mint. Season lightly with salt and pepper. Use a pair of scissors to snip the sun-dried tomatoes into thin strips, sprinkling them evenly over the breads. Top with the brie, laying the wedges cut sides down, with the rind up.

Drizzle a little oil over the brie and place under the grill for 2–4 minutes, until the rind is browned and the cheese runny. Stir the Greek yogurt and spoon a little on the breads. Garnish with the reserved mint sprigs and serve immediately.

ingredients

200–225 g/7–8 oz wedge of brie, chilled in the freezer

6 fresh mint sprigs

2 pitta breads

$1/4$ cucumber (about 7 cm/ 3 inches), thinly sliced

salt and pepper

10 sun-dried tomatoes in oil, drained (about 50 g/2 oz)

olive oil

2 tbsp Greek yogurt

Salami, Pepper & Pine Nut Panini

serves 2

Preheat the grill to a medium–high setting. Lay a piece of cooking foil on the rack in the grill pan. Mix the pepper strips and garlic in a heap on the foil. Drizzle with a little olive oil, turn the strips to coat them lightly and then spread them out.

Lay the bread halves cut sides down on the foil around the pepper strips. Cook for about 1 minute to lightly toast the breads, then remove them and continue cooking the pepper strips for 2–3 minutes or until they begin to brown.

Replace the breads on the foil, cut sides up. Cover the bottom layers of bread with the salami and basil leaves. Add the pepper strips and sprinkle with the pine nuts. Cut the radicchio into wedges and arrange them on top. Drizzle with a little oil and grill for 2–3 minutes, until beginning to wilt and brown at the edges. Remove the top layers of bread as soon as they are toasted.

Sprinkle with Parmesan or pecorino, add the bread tops and serve immediately.

ingredients

1 large red pepper, deseeded and cut into thin strips

2 garlic cloves, sliced

olive oil

2 panini rolls or individual ciabatta, split horizontally

6 salami slices

handful of fresh basil leaves

1 tbsp pine nuts

1 small head radicchio or chicory

Parmesan or pecorino shavings

Mozzarella-grilled Panini with Chilli-Spiked Prawns & Olives

serves 2

Preheat the grill to a medium–high setting. Dry the prawns on kitchen paper and place them in a bowl. Add the chilli, spring onions, olives and garlic, if liked. Stir in the lemon rind and juice, parsley and seasoning to taste.

Slice the bread into two layers and place the bottom halves, cut sides down, on the rack in the grill pan. Lay the top halves on the rack, cut sides up. Toast the breads for 1–2 minutes until browned and crisp.

Turn the breads over. Divide the prawn mixture between the bottom halves, piling it in place and making sure the breads are covered. Arrange the mozzarella slices on the top halves. Drizzle a hint of olive oil over the prawn mixture and on the mozzarella but take care not to add too much or the bread will be greasy.

Place under the grill until the prawn filling is hot and the mozzarella is melted and bubbling. Use a palette knife to lift the bread lids on top of the prawn filling, scraping up any mozzarella that may have drizzled off the bread. Serve immediately.

ingredients

225 g/8 oz peeled cooked prawns, thawed if frozen

1 fresh green chilli, deseeded and chopped

2 spring onions, chopped

50 g/2 oz pitted black olives, halved

1 garlic clove, chopped (optional)

grated rind of 1 lemon and squeeze of lemon juice

small handful of parsley, trimmed and roughly chopped

2 panini rolls or individual ciabatta

salt and pepper

150 g/5 oz mozzarella cheese, thinly sliced

olive oil

Chorizo &
Fennel Crostini

serves 4

Preheat the grill to a medium setting. Cover the rack in the grill pan with a piece of cooking foil. Place the slices of bread on the foil and brush with olive oil. Toast for about 3 minutes, until crisp and golden.

Meanwhile, shred the fennel finely. Mix the fennel and onion with seasoning and a little olive oil in a bowl, adding just enough oil to moisten the vegetables. Separate the onion into curvy strips as you mix. Cut the top and bottom off the grapefruit, then cut off all the rind and pith working down around the sides. Cut out the segments from between the membranes. Turn the bread over, brush with olive oil and cover with the fennel mixture. Grill for a further 3 minutes, until the vegetables are lightly cooked and beginning to brown.

Increase the heat to the hottest setting. Top the breads with grapefruit segments and then cover with slices of chorizo. Brush or drizzle with a little olive oil and grill for about 1 minute, until the chorizo is sizzling, curling a little and beginning to brown.

Top with crème fraîche, sprinkle with chopped fresh coriander and serve immediately.

ingredients

12 slices French bread (about 2.5 cm /1 inch thick)

olive oil

1 fennel bulb

1 red onion, halved and thinly sliced

salt and pepper

1 pink grapefruit

24 thin slices chorizo (about 125 g/$4^{1}/_{2}$ oz)

4 tbsp crème fraîche

2 tbsp chopped fresh coriander leaves

Sausage &
Mushroom Brioche

serves 2–4

Use a vegetable peeler to pare the carrots into fine strips. Place in a bowl of cold water, then add ice and set aside for about 30 minutes.

Preheat the grill to a medium–high setting. Grill the sausages for about 15 minutes, turning once or twice, until browned and almost cooked.

In a bowl, mix together the tarragon, garlic, oil and orange rind and juice. Mix half the dressing with the mushrooms then toast the brioche lightly on both sides in a toaster.

Increase the heat to the hottest setting. Place the brioche on the rack in the grill pan. Cover with mushrooms up to the edges of the bread (otherwise it will burn). Grill close to the heat source for 2–4 minutes until lightly cooked.

Slice the sausages and arrange them on the mushrooms. Grill well away from the heat for about 5 minutes, until the sausages are browned.

Drain the carrots. Arrange the lamb's lettuce or salad on plates and drizzle with the remaining dressing. Add the toasts and top with the carrot curls. Serve immediately.

ingredients

2 large carrots

4 fresh chunky Italian or Toulouse sausages (about 450 g/1 lb)

6 fresh tarragon sprigs, leaves only

1 garlic clove, chopped

4 tbsp olive oil

grated rind and juice of 1 orange

200 g/7 oz open chestnut mushrooms or shiitake, thickly sliced

4 thick slices of good brioche loaf (plain, not sweetened or flavoured with vanilla)

lamb's lettuce or other salad leaves, to serve

Brunch
Bruschetta

serves 2

Preheat the grill to a medium setting. Lay the ciabatta on the rack in the grill pan. Grill until lightly browned, then turn and cook on the other side. Reserve and keep warm.

Mix the tomato, spring onions, cheese, avocado, balsamic vinegar and half of the oil together in a medium bowl. Season to taste with salt and pepper.

Drizzle the remaining oil over the ciabatta toast and top with the tomato mixture. Garnish with the basil and serve immediately.

ingredients

4 slices ciabatta bread

1 large ripe tomato, diced

2 spring onions, finely sliced

1 small fresh buffalo mozzarella cheese, diced

$1/2$ ripe avocado, diced

$1/2$ tbsp balsamic vinegar

2 tbsp extra virgin olive oil

salt and pepper

2 tbsp shredded fresh basil leaves, to garnish

Basque Scrambled Eggs

serves 4–6

Preheat the grill to a medium–high setting. Lay the bread on the rack in the grill pan. Toast until lightly browned, then turn and cook on the other side. Keep warm.

Heat 2 tablespoons of oil in a large, heavy-based frying pan over a medium–high heat. Add the onion and peppers and cook for about 5 minutes, or until the vegetables are soft, but not brown. Add the tomatoes and heat through. Transfer to a plate and keep warm in a preheated low oven.

Add another tablespoon of oil to the frying pan. Add the chorizo and cook for 30 seconds, just to warm through and flavour the oil. Add the sausage to the reserved vegetables.

There should be about 2 tablespoons of oil in the frying pan but add a little extra, if necessary, to make up the amount. Add the butter and allow to melt. Season the eggs with salt and pepper to taste, then add to the frying pan and scramble until cooked to the desired degree of firmness. Return the vegetables to the frying pan and stir through. Serve at once with the hot toast.

ingredients

4–6 thick slices country-style bread

olive oil

1 large onion, chopped finely

1 large red pepper, cored, deseeded and chopped

1 large green pepper, cored, deseeded and chopped

2 large tomatoes, peeled, deseeded and chopped

55 g/2 oz chorizo sausage, sliced thinly, casings removed, if preferred

35 g/1$^{1}/_{4}$ oz butter

10 large eggs, beaten lightly

salt and pepper

Bagels with Leeks & Cheese

serves 2

Preheat the grill to a medium setting. Lay the bagels cut side up on the rack in the grill pan. Toast until lightly browned, then reserve and keep warm. Do not turn the grill off.

Trim the leeks, discarding the green ends, and split down the middle, leaving the root intact. Wash well to remove any grit and slice finely, discarding the root.

Melt the butter over a low heat in a large sauté pan and add the leeks. Cook, stirring constantly, for 5 minutes, or until the leeks are soft and slightly browned. Leave to cool.

Mix the cooled leeks, grated cheese, spring onions, parsley and salt and pepper to taste together. Spread the cheese mixture over the top of each bagel and place under the grill until bubbling and golden brown.

ingredients

2 fresh bagels

2 leeks

25 g/1 oz butter

125 g/$4^1/_2$ oz grated Gruyère cheese

2 spring onions, finely chopped

1 tbsp chopped fresh parsley

salt and pepper

Cheese & Sun-dried
Tomato Toasts

serves 4

Preheat the grill to a medium–high setting and preheat the oven to 220°C/425°F/ Gas Mark 7. Slice the loaves diagonally and discard the end pieces. Place the slices of bread on the rack in the grill pan and toast on both sides until golden.

Spread one side of each toast with the sun-dried tomato paste and top with mozzarella. Sprinkle with oregano and season to taste with pepper.

Put the toasts on a large baking sheet and drizzle with oil. Bake in the preheated oven for 5 minutes, or until the cheese is melted and bubbling. Remove the toasts from the oven and leave to stand for 5 minutes before serving.

ingredients

2 small baguettes

175 ml/6 fl oz sun-dried tomato paste

300 g/$10^1/_2$ oz buffalo mozzarella cheese, drained and diced

$1^1/_2$ tsp dried oregano

pepper

2–3 tbsp olive oil

Mushroom Bruschetta

serves 4

Preheat the grill to a medium–high setting. Place the slices on the rack in the grill pan and toast on both sides until golden. Reserve and keep warm.

Meanwhile, heat the oil in a frying pan. Add the garlic and cook gently for a few seconds, then add the chestnut mushrooms. Cook, stirring constantly, over a high heat for 3 minutes. Add the wild mushrooms and cook for a further 2 minutes. Stir in the lemon juice.

Season to taste with salt and pepper and stir in the chopped parsley.

Spoon the mushroom mixture on to the warm toast and serve.

ingredients

12 slices baguette, each 1 cm/ ^{1}/$_2$ inch thick, or 2 individual baguettes, cut lengthways

3 tbsp olive oil

2 garlic cloves, crushed

225 g/8 oz chestnut mushrooms, sliced

225 g/8 oz mixed wild mushrooms

2 tsp lemon juice

salt and pepper

2 tbsp chopped fresh parsley

Grilled Feta Cheese with
Chilli on Ciabatta Toast

serves 2

Preheat the grill to a medium–high setting. Place the slices of bread on the rack in the grill pan and toast on both sides until golden. Cover each bread slice with a generous slice of feta cheese. Mix the oil, chilli flakes and oregano together and drizzle evenly over the cheese.

Cook under the preheated grill for 2–3 minutes, or until the cheese begins to melt, and place on serving plates. Drizzle over a little extra oil and serve with rocket leaves.

ingredients

4 slices ciabatta bread

200 g/7 oz feta cheese

2 tbsp olive oil, plus extra for drizzling

1 tsp dried chilli flakes

1 tsp dried oregano

85 g/3 oz rocket leaves, to serve

Quick & Easy Lunches

Perfect Grilled Cheese Sandwich

serves 4

Slice the crusty top off the loaf; reserve for another use. Slice the loaf into two layers, making the bottom thicker. Place the bottom on a large piece of cooking foil.

Preheat the grill to a medium–high setting. Toast the top surface of the top layer of the loaf until brown, then turn it and place on the foil.

Sprinkle cheese over both layers of bread. Arrange avocado and tomato wedges on the bottom layer then sprinkle with half the remaining cheese. Top with the asparagus spears and ham, completely covering the edges of the ingredients underneath. Sprinkle with the remaining cheese, pepper to taste and a trickle of olive oil.

Cook well away from the heat source for 3–5 minutes. Remove the plain cheese-topped layer first, when the cheese is bubbling. Cook the bottom layer until the cheese has melted and the ham is browned.

Cut the toasted cheese layer into 8 wedges and overlap them on the filling, alternating the plain and cheese sides up. Serve at once, cut into four wedges.

ingredients

1 stoneground buckwheat boule loaf (about 17.5 cm/7 inches in diameter) or other rustic round loaf

175 g/6 oz Cheddar cheese, finely shaved or coarsely grated

1 large avocado, halved, stoned, peeled and sliced

2 tomatoes, halved and cut into fine wedges

12 asparagus spears, cooked, bottled or canned

4 slices Parma, Serrano or Black Forest ham

pepper

olive oil

Smoked Chicken & Ham Focaccia

serves 2–4

Preheat a griddle plate or pan under the grill until both grill and griddle are hot. If you do not have a griddle, heat a heavy baking sheet or shallow roasting tin. Slice the thick focaccia in half horizontally and cut the top half into strips. If using slightly thinner flatbread, leave one whole and slice the second bread into strips.

Cover the bottom half of the focaccia (or whole bread) with basil leaves, top with the courgettes in an even layer and then cover with the chicken and ham, alternating the slices and wrinkling them. Lay the strips of focaccia on top, placing strips of taleggio cheese between them. Sprinkle with a little nutmeg if liked.

Place the assembled bread on the hot griddle and cook under the grill, well away from the heat, for about 5 minutes, until the taleggio has melted and the top of the bread is browned. Serve immediately with cherry tomatoes if liked, cutting the bread into four across the strips.

ingredients

1 thick focaccia loaf (about 15–17.5 cm/6–7 inches in diameter) or 2 Italian flatbreads

handful of basil leaves

2 small courgettes, coarsely grated

6 paper-thin slices smoked chicken

6 paper-thin slices cooked ham

225 g/8 oz taleggio cheese, cut into strips

freshly grated nutmeg (optional)

cherry tomatoes, to serve (optional)

Roast Pepper Ciabatta with Chopped Eggs & Olives

serves 2–4

Place the eggs in a small pan, add hot water to cover and bring to the boil. Reduce the heat and simmer for 8 minutes. Drain, rinse under cold water and shell the eggs, then chop them and place in a bowl. Add the olives and coriander with seasoning to taste, fork the ingredients together and set aside.

Mix the red, green and yellow pepper strips together in a bowl, then mix the onion, garlic, oregano and olive oil in a separate bowl. Season the onion mixture, to taste.

Slice the ciabatta in half horizontally. Place cut sides down on the rack in a grill pan and toast the tops for about a minute, until crisp and lightly browned. Turn the bread. Arrange the pepper strips on the bread, covering it completely. Sprinkle the onion, garlic and oregano over as you go and drizzle any remaining oil over.

Grill the pepper-topped ciabatta for 4–5 minutes, until the peppers are softened and well browned in places. Top with the egg mixture and add lemon wedges so that their juice can be sprinkled over. Serve immediately.

ingredients

2 eggs

50 g/2 oz pitted black olives, chopped

2 tbsp chopped fresh coriander leaves

salt and pepper

1 large red pepper, deseeded and cut into thin strips

1 large green pepper, deseeded and cut into thin strips

1 large yellow pepper, deseeded and cut into thin strips

1 small red onion, finely chopped

1 garlic clove, finely chopped

1 tbsp chopped fresh oregano

2 tbsp olive oil

1 large ciabatta loaf

lemon wedges, to serve

Tempting Tomato
Bruschetta

serves 4

Mix the tomato purée, mustard, garlic, sugar and vinegar in a bowl large enough to hold all the other ingredients. Whisk in 2 tbsp of the oil until thoroughly combined.

Preheat the grill on the hottest setting. Place the slices of bread on the rack in the grill pan and brush lightly with oil, then toast until crisp and golden.

Meanwhile, add the spring onions, thyme and parsley to the tomato mixture and mix thoroughly. Stir in the diced tomatoes until they are thoroughly combined with the other ingredients. Add seasoning to taste.

Turn the bread slices and cover the untoasted sides with the tomato mixture, using a teaspoon to nudge the tomatoes and their juices right up to the edges. Slide the bruschetta close together and cook under the grill, not too close to the heat, for 4–5 minutes, until lightly browned in places.

Transfer to a platter, garnish with herb sprigs and drizzle with a hint of olive oil. Serve at once.

ingredients

2 tbsp tomato purée

1 tbsp mustard, such as Dijon or wholegrain

2 garlic cloves, crushed

1/2 tsp sugar

1 tbsp cider vinegar

about 4 tbsp extra virgin olive oil, plus extra for serving

12 slices good French bread

4 spring onions, chopped

2 tbsp fresh thyme leaves

handful of chopped parsley, stalks discarded

6 tomatoes, diced

salt and pepper

Salad Greek Crostini

serves 2

Preheat the grill to a medium–high setting. Mix the garlic and olive oil in a bowl large enough to mix all the salad ingredients.

Place the bread on the rack in the grill pan. Brush lightly with the garlic oil and toast well away from the heat for 2–3 minutes, until crisp and golden. Turn the bread and brush lightly with more oil, then toast again.

Add the feta cheese to the garlic oil remaining in the bowl and season with pepper (the cheese and olives usually provide enough salt). Mix in the cucumber, olives, tomatoes, onion, mint and oregano. Sprinkle with the sugar and mix well. Finally, lightly mix in the lettuce.

Transfer the crostini to plates and spoon the salad and its juices over them. Sprinkle with the sesame seeds and pine kernels, if liked, and serve immediately, while the crostini are hot and crisp.

ingredients

1 garlic clove, crushed

4 tbsp olive oil

2 thick slices of a large bloomer with sesame seeds

200 g/7 oz feta cheese, diced

pepper

1/4 cucumber, finely diced

25 g/1 oz black olives, sliced

4 plum tomatoes, diced

1/2 small onion, chopped

2 sprigs fresh mint leaves, shredded

2 sprigs fresh oregano leaves, chopped

1/4 tsp sugar

1 heart Little Gem lettuce, finely shredded

1/2 tsp toasted sesame seeds

2 tsp pine kernels (optional)

Sherried Chicken & Bacon Toasts

serves 2

Heat the oil in a frying pan and add the bacon, onion, garlic, bay leaf and thyme. Cook, stirring often, for 5 minutes, until the bacon and onion are cooked. Add the chicken and continue cooking for 5 minutes, stirring so that the chicken cooks evenly.

Add the mustard and sherry and bring to the boil, stirring all the sediment off the bottom of the pan. Add seasoning to taste. Simmer for 3–4 minutes, until the sherry is reduced to a mustard-glaze on the ingredients. Discard the bay leaf and herb sprigs.

Meanwhile, preheat the grill to a medium–high setting and warm two plates. Place the bread on a rack in the grill pan and toast for about 2 minutes on each side, until evenly golden and crisp.

Butter the hot toast and place on the warmed plates. Stir the parsley into the chicken mixture and pile it on the toasts. Drizzle over a little yogurt, if liked, then serve immediately.

ingredients

2 tbsp olive oil

2 rindless bacon rashers, cut into strips

1 small onion, chopped

2 garlic cloves, chopped

1 bay leaf

2 fresh thyme sprigs

2 small boneless skinless chicken breasts, cut into small chunks

1 tbsp wholegrain mustard

6 tbsp dry sherry

salt and pepper

2 slices traditional white bread, 1.5 cm/$3/4$ inch thick

about 25 g/1 oz butter, softened

small handful of chopped parsley, stalks discarded

2 tbsp mild plain yogurt (optional)

Rye Toast with
Roast Beef & Coleslaw

serves 1

Preheat the grill to a medium–high setting. Mix the ginger with the butter.

Spread one slice of bread generously with the butter. Top with the cabbage, trimming any overhanging shreds and placing them back on the middle of the sandwich. Top with grated carrot and spring onion, keeping them away from the edge. Season lightly.

Spread a little of the butter on one side of the beef and lay it, butter down, on the carrot. Spread the remaining butter on the second slice of bread and place it on top of the sandwich, buttered side down.

Toast the sandwich on the rack in the grill pan on both sides, until crisp and golden. Serve at once with dill pickles, if liked.

ingredients

1 tbsp finely chopped fresh root ginger or horseradish sauce

20 g/$^3/_4$ oz butter, softened

2 slices light rye bread, preferably with caraway

1 very thin slice cabbage (white or firm green heart)

1 small carrot, coarsely grated

1 spring onion, sliced

1 large slice roast beef

salt and pepper

dill pickles, to serve (optional)

Turkey
Ciabatta with Walnuts

serves 2

Preheat the grill to a medium–high setting. Slice the ciabatta rolls in half horizontally and toast the cut sides on the rack in the grill pan. Remove the top layers. Turn the bottom layers and toast the undersides until brown and crisp. When the breads are toasted, reduce the heat to a low setting.

Meanwhile, mix the blue cheese, walnuts and sage. Lay the turkey slices on the bases of the rolls and top with the cheese and walnut mixture, piling it up in the middle. Cover with the tops of the rolls.

Heat the rolls under the grill, well away from the heat, for 3–4 minutes, until the breads are hot and the cheese is beginning to melt. Increase the heat slightly, if necessary, to a medium setting but do not turn it up high enough to brown the tops of the rolls before they are warmed through.

Serve the hot rolls with green grapes as an accompaniment.

ingredients

2 ciabatta rolls

100 g/4 oz blue cheese, such as Stilton or Danish blue, finely diced or crumbled

100 g/4 oz walnuts, chopped

8 large fresh sage leaves, finely shredded

4 slices cooked turkey breast

seedless green grapes, to serve

Cake Toasts
Crab

serves 4

Place one piece of bread on a plate and spoon the milk evenly over it. Leave to stand for a few minutes. Brush the remaining slices lightly on both sides with butter.

Mix the crabmeat, chilli and spring onion in a bowl. Mash the soaked bread with a fork and mix it with the crabmeat, scraping in the milk off the plate. Stir in the remaining melted butter and seasoning to taste.

Preheat the grill to a medium–high setting and toast the buttered bread on the rack in the grill pan, until crisp and golden on both sides. Top with the crab mixture, spreading it evenly right over the edges and forking the surface slightly so that it is not too smooth.

Place under the grill for about 3 minutes, until the creamy topping is browned. Cut into quarters and serve at once with lemon wedges for squeezing over the crab.

ingredients

3 slices good white bread, crusts removed

2 tbsp milk

50 g/2 oz butter, melted

170 g/6 oz canned crabmeat, drained, or 150 g/5 oz fresh or frozen crabmeat, thawed if frozen

1 green chilli, deseeded and chopped

1 spring onion, finely chopped

salt and pepper

lemon wedges, to serve

Tuscan Beans on Ciabatta Toast with Fresh Herbs

serves 2

Preheat the grill to a medium setting. Lay the ciabatta on the rack in the grill pan. Grill until lightly browned, then turn and cook on the other side. Reserve and keep warm.

Heat the oil in a medium sauté pan and cook the onion over a low heat until soft. Add the garlic and cook for a further 1 minute, then add the butter beans, water and tomato purée. Bring to the boil, stirring occasionally, and cook for 2 minutes.

Add the balsamic vinegar, parsley and basil and stir to combine. Season to taste with salt and pepper and serve over slices of the toasted ciabatta.

ingredients

2 thick slices ciabatta

1 tbsp olive oil

1 small onion, finely diced

1 garlic clove, crushed

250 g/9 oz canned butter beans, drained and rinsed

90 ml/3 fl oz water

1 tbsp tomato purée

1 tsp balsamic vinegar

1 tbsp chopped fresh parsley

1 tbsp torn fresh basil

salt and pepper

Something Special

Salmon &
Watercress Ciabatta

serves 2

Preheat the grill to a medium–high setting. Slice the ciabatta
in half horizontally and place cut sides down on the rack in the
grill pan. Toast until browned.

Cut the salmon fillet into 1-cm/$1/2$-inch thick slices and place
in a large shallow flameproof dish. Sprinkle the lime rind and
juice over. Season well and trickle the oil over. Cook the salmon
under the hot grill for 2 minutes. Turn the slices and cook for
2 minutes, until the fish is firm and cooked. Remove and set
aside. Spoon some of the juices from the salmon evenly over
the cut sides of the bread, then place under the grill and toast
for about 2 minutes, until crisp and golden.

Spread half the watercress over the bottom half of the bread.
Sprinkle with the capers. Arrange the salmon slices on top,
overlapping them slightly. Then spoon the remaining cooking
juices over. Sprinkle with the chives and top with the remaining
watercress. Replace the top of the loaf, cut the ciabatta into
four slices and serve immediately.

ingredients

1 large ciabatta

250 g/9 oz skinless boneless
salmon fillet

grated rind of 1 lime or lemon and
juice of $1/2$ lime or lemon

salt and pepper

2 tbsp olive oil

large bag of watercress, tough
stalks discarded

1 tbsp capers

2 tbsp snipped fresh chives

Toasted Aubergine & Anchovy
Focaccia with Goat's Cheese

serves 4

Preheat the grill to a medium–high setting. Slice the bread in half horizontally and lay on the rack in the grill pan. Toast the underside of the bottom layer, and cut side of the top layer, for about 2 minutes, until browned.

Drain and reserve the oil from the anchovies. Remove the bread and lay the aubergine slices on the rack. Brush with the reserved oil and grill for 4–5 minutes, until well browned.

Chop the anchovies and mix with the spring onions. Arrange the aubergines and cheese on the bread, covering the untoasted surfaces of the bottom and the top of the loaf (or the tops of both flatbreads). Top with the anchovy mixture. Brush the remaining oil lightly over the aubergine. Grill for 3–4 minutes, until browned.

Purée the basil, coriander, lemon rind and olive oil in a blender. Top the bottom layer of bread with tomatoes and add the second layer on top, aubergines up. Cut into wedges. Serve drizzled with the herb oil.

ingredients

1 thick focaccia loaf (about 15 cm/ 6 inches) or 2 Italian flatbreads

50 g/2 oz canned anchovies in olive oil

1 aubergine, about 250 g/9 oz, thinly sliced

6 spring onions, chopped

150 g/5 oz goat's cheese, thinly sliced

handful of basil leaves

handful of fresh coriander leaves

grated rind of 1 lemon

4 tbsp olive oil

10–12 cherry tomatoes, halved

Creamy Pan-glazed Pork with Grapes on Walnut Toasts

serves 2–4

Mix the grapes with the lime rind and a squeeze of juice, and set aside. Preheat the grill to a medium–high setting. Trim the crusts off the bread. Heat the olive oil and butter in a large frying pan until the butter has melted. Remove from the heat. Brush both sides of the bread slices sparingly with some of the butter and oil.

Toast the bread on the rack in the grill pan for 2 minutes on each side. Cut each toast into four and keep hot in the warm grill. Meanwhile, add the garlic, bay leaf and rosemary to the oil in the pan and heat. Add the onion and stir-fry for about 2 minutes, until soft but not browned. Add the pork and fry over fairly high heat for 3–4 minutes, stirring frequently, until lightly browned.

Add the celery with seasoning and stir-fry for 2–3 minutes until the celery is lightly cooked and the pork well browned. Discard the herbs. Place the toasts on plates. Top with the pork, using a slotted spoon. Keep hot.

Replace the pan on the heat, add the brandy and cook over high heat, scraping all the cooking juices off the pan. Boil hard for about a minute. Add the cream and bring to the boil, stirring. Remove from the heat and stir in the parsley. Drizzle over the pork. Add the grapes and serve.

ingredients

175 g/6 oz seedless green grapes, halved

zested rind of 1 lime and a squeeze of juice

4 slices walnut bread

2 tbsp olive oil

25 g/1 oz butter

1 garlic clove, chopped

1 bay leaf

1 rosemary sprig

1 small onion, halved and sliced

350 g/12 oz lean pork strips

2 celery sticks, very thinly sliced

salt and pepper

4 tbsp brandy

125 ml/4 fl oz double cream

2 tbsp chopped fresh parsley

Avocado
Prawn Toasts

serves 4

Finely chop the prawns in a food processor. Add the cornflour, egg white and seasoning, and pulse once or twice to mix to a coarse paste. Do not over-process the mixture or it will become too thin. Transfer to a bowl and mix in the lemon rind, celery, parsley and chives.

Preheat the grill to a medium–high setting. Brush the bread lightly with butter on both sides and toast on the rack in the grill pan for 2 minutes on each side. The pan must not be too near the heat.

Reduce the heat to medium–low. Trim the very edges of the crusts off the toasts and divide the prawn mixture between them, spreading it out evenly to cover the bread completely. Grill for 1 minute, until the mixture is lightly set, then brush with the remaining butter. Cook for 3–4 minutes, until set and golden.

Halve, stone, peel and dice the avocados. Whisk the lemon juice with the mustard, tarragon and seasoning. Gradually whisk in the oil.

Cut the cooked toasts into quarters and place on warmed plates. Top with the avocado, the lemon dressing, and garnish with the tarragon sprigs and serve.

ingredients

225 g/8 oz peeled cooked prawns, thawed if frozen and drained

2 tbsp cornflour

1 egg white

salt and pepper

grated rind of 1 lemon

1 celery stick, finely chopped

2 tbsp chopped fresh parsley

4 tbsp snipped fresh chives

4 medium slices of good white bread

50 g/2 oz butter, melted

2 avocados

1 tbsp lemon juice

$1/2$ tsp Dijon mustard (or other type, to taste)

1 tbsp tarragon

3 tbsp olive oil

fresh tarragon sprigs, to garnish

Glazed Beetroot & Egg Sourdough Toasties

serves 2–4

Boil the eggs for 8 minutes, then drain, shell and chop them. Set aside. Dice the beetroot into quite small pieces and place in a small bowl. Mix in half the sugar, 1 tsp of the cider vinegar and seasoning.

Preheat the grill to a medium–high setting. Brush the bread with a little olive oil and toast on the rack in the grill pan for 2–3 minutes, until crisp and golden.

Meanwhile, trickle 1 tsp of the remaining oil over the beetroot. Whisk the remaining cider vinegar, mustard and remaining sugar together with seasoning. Gradually whisk in the remaining oil to make a thick dressing. Stir in the dill and taste for seasoning – it should be sweet and mustardy, with a sharpness – add more sugar or vinegar if you wish.

Turn the bread and top with the beetroot, giving it a stir first, covering the slices right up to the crusts. Glaze the beetroot under the grill for 2–3 minutes, until browned in places.

Cut the slices in half or quarters and top with egg. Drizzle with a little dressing, garnish with the dill sprigs and serve immediately.

ingredients

4 eggs

500 g/1 lb 2 oz cooked beetroot (fresh or vacuum-packed without vinegar)

2 tsp sugar

5 tsp cider vinegar

salt and pepper

6 tbsp olive oil

1 tbsp Dijon mustard

3 tbsp chopped fresh dill

4 slices sourdough bread (from a long oval loaf)

dill sprigs, to garnish

Italian Steak Heroes

serves 4

Heat the olive oil in a large saucepan over a medium heat, add the onion, garlic, pepper and mushrooms and cook, stirring occasionally, for 5–10 minutes until softened and beginning to brown.

Add the mince and cook, stirring frequently and breaking up any lumps with a wooden spoon, for 5 minutes, or until well browned. Add the wine, tomato purée and salt and pepper to taste and leave to simmer for 10 minutes, stirring occasionally. Remove from the heat.

Split the ciabatta rolls in half and brush both halves with extra virgin olive oil. Put the bottom halves onto a piece of foil and spoon an equal quantity of the sauce on top of each.

Slice the cheese, then divide between the roll bottoms and arrange on top of the sauce. Add the basil leaves and cover with the tops of the rolls. Press down gently and grill under a low heat, for 5-10 minutes or until golden. Leave the sandwiches for at least 1 hour before serving.

ingredients

1 tbsp olive oil

1 small onion, finely chopped

1 garlic clove, finely chopped

1 small red pepper, cored, deseeded and finely chopped

100 g/$3^1/_2$ oz button mushrooms, finely chopped

200 g/7 oz fresh steak mince

125 ml/4 fl oz red wine

2 tbsp tomato purée

salt and pepper

4 ciabatta rolls

extra virgin olive oil, for brushing

75 g/$2^3/_4$ oz mozzarella cheese

2 tbsp torn fresh basil leaves

Pear & Roquefort
Open-face Sandwiches

serves 2–4

Preheat the grill to a medium–high setting. Toast the bread slices on the rack in the grill pan until crisp, but not brown, on both sides. Do not turn off the grill.

Fold or cut the ham slices to cover each slice of bread, then equally divide the pear slices between the breads. Lay the cheese slices on top.

Return the breads to the grill until the cheese melts and bubbles. Serve.

ingredients

4 slices walnut bread or pain Poilâne, about 1 cm/^{1}/$_2$ inch thick

4 thin slices cured ham, such as Bayonne or Parma

2 ripe pears, such as Conference, peeled, halved, cored and thinly sliced lengthways

100 g/3^1/$_2$ oz Roquefort cheese, very thinly sliced

Focaccia with Roasted Cherry Tomatoes, Basil & Crispy Pancetta

serves 4–6

Place the flour, dried basil, sugar, yeast and salt in a large bowl. Combine the water and oil and mix with the dry ingredients to form a soft dough, adding more water if the dough appears too dry. Turn out on to a lightly floured work surface and knead for 10 minutes, or until the dough bounces back when pressed lightly with your finger. Place the dough in a lightly oiled bowl and cover with clingfilm. Leave in a warm place for 1 hour, or until doubled in size.

Meanwhile, preheat the oven to 140°C/275°F/Gas Mark 1. Place the tomatoes on a baking tray covered with baking paper, sprinkle with oil and season to taste with salt and pepper. Bake for 30 minutes, or until the tomatoes are soft. Increase the oven temperature to 220°C/425°F/Gas Mark 7. Remove the dough from the bowl and knead again briefly. Shape into a rectangle and place on a lightly oiled baking tray, turning the dough over to oil both sides. Make rough indentations in the dough using your fingers. Top with the tomatoes and pancetta. Sprinkle with salt and pepper. Leave in a warm place for 10 minutes for the dough to rise again. Bake for 15–20 minutes, or until golden brown and cooked through. Drizzle with oil and top with fresh basil. Serve warm.

ingredients

500 g/1 lb 2 oz strong white bread flour, plus extra for kneading and rolling

1 tbsp dried basil

1/2 tsp sugar

2 tsp easy-blend dried yeast

2 tsp salt

325 ml/11 fl oz water, lukewarm

2 tbsp olive oil, plus extra for oiling

topping

400 g/14 oz cherry tomatoes

1 tbsp olive oil, plus extra for oiling and drizzling

salt and pepper

200 g/7 oz thick pancetta, diced

4 tbsp chopped fresh basil

Double Chocolate
Mango Brioche

serves 4

Preheat the grill to a medium–high setting. Toast the brioche slices on the rack in the grill pan, on both sides, until crisp and browned. Remove and leave to cool for a couple of minutes on a rack.

Increase the heat to the hottest setting and lay a piece of cooking foil on the rack in the grill pan. Trim off and discard the edges of the crusts from the toasts. Spread the toasts generously with chocolate spread, as thick as you prefer, taking it right up to the edges.

Place the toasts on the foil. Arrange the mango slices on top and sprinkle the sugar over them. Sprinkle with the lime rind and juice. Cook for 1–2 minutes – just long enough to melt the sugar and make the fruit and its dressing hot on the surface.

Top with chocolate ice cream and crème fraîche, decorate with lime slices, if liked, and serve immediately.

ingredients

4 thick slices brioche loaf (about 2.5–3.5 cm/1–1^1/$_2$ inches thick)

3–4 tbsp good-quality chocolate spread

1 large mango, peeled, stoned and thinly sliced

4 tsp sugar

grated rind and juice of 1 lime

4 scoops good-quality dark chocolate ice cream

4 tbsp crème fraîche or Greek yogurt

lime slices, to decorate (optional)

Spiced French Toast
with Seasonal Berries

serves 4

Preheat the oven to 220°C/425°F/Gas Mark 7. Put the eggs and egg white in a large, shallow bowl or dish and whisk together with a fork. Add the cinnamon and mixed spice and whisk until combined.

To prepare the berry topping, put the sugar and orange juice in a saucepan and bring to the boil over a low heat, stirring until the sugar has dissolved. Add the berries, remove from the heat and leave to cool for 10 minutes.

Meanwhile, soak the bread slices in the egg mixture for about 1 minute on each side. Brush a large baking sheet with the melted butter and place the bread slices on the sheet. Bake in the preheated oven for 5–7 minutes, or until lightly browned. Turn the slices over and bake for a further 2–3 minutes. Serve the berries spooned over the toast and decorate with mint sprigs.

ingredients

4 eggs, plus 1 extra egg white

1/4 tsp ground cinnamon

1/4 tsp mixed spice

4 slices thick white bread

1 tbsp butter, melted

fresh mint sprigs, to decorate

berry topping

85 g/3 oz caster sugar

50 ml/2 fl oz freshly squeezed orange juice

300 g/10 1/2 oz mixed fresh seasonal berries, such as strawberries, raspberries and blueberries, picked over and hulled

anchovies: toasted aubergine & anchovy focaccia
    with goat's cheese 79
asparagus: perfect grilled cheese sandwich 54
aubergines: toasted aubergine & anchovy focaccia
    with goat's cheese 79
avocados
    avocado prawn toasts 83
    brunch bruschetta 41
    perfect grilled cheese sandwich 54

bacon
    sherried chicken & bacon toasts 65
    toasted English muffins with blueberries & bacon 17
    toasted English muffins with honey-glazed bacon & eggs 22
bagels
    bagels with leeks & cheese 45
    hot smoked salmon, tomato & cream cheese bagel 13
beef
    Italian steak heroes 87
    rye toast with roast beef & coleslaw 66
beetroot: glazed beetroot & egg sourdough toasties 84
berries
    spiced French toast with seasonal berries 95
    toasted English muffins with blueberries & bacon 17
bread 6
    avocado prawn toasts 83
    Basque scrambled eggs 42
    cheese & sun-dried tomato toasts 46
    chorizo & fennel crostini 37
    crab cake toasts 70
    croque monsieur 25
    French toast with maple syrup 21
    Greek salad crostini 62
    mushroom bruschetta 49
    perfect grilled cheese sandwich 54
    sherried chicken & bacon toasts 65
    spiced French toast with seasonal berries 95
    tempting tomato bruschetta 61
    toast, perfect 10
    toasted cheese sandwich with egg 14
    see also specific varieties of bread
brioche
    chive scrambled eggs with brioche 26
    double chocolate mango brioche 92
    sausage & mushroom brioche 38
butter beans: Tuscan beans on ciabatta toast
    with fresh herbs 73

cabbage: rye toast with roast beef & coleslaw 66
capers: salmon & watercress ciabatta 76
cheese
    bagels with leeks & cheese 45
    brunch bruschetta 41
    croque monsieur 25
    ham & cheese croissant 18
    hot smoked salmon, tomato & cream cheese bagel 13
    minted summer brie on pitta 30
    pear & Roquefort open-face sandwiches 88
    perfect grilled cheese sandwich 54
    salami, pepper & pine nut panini 33
    smoked chicken & ham focaccia 57
    toasted aubergine & anchovy focaccia with goat's cheese 79
    toasted cheese sandwich with egg 14
    turkey ciabatta with walnuts 69
    see also feta cheese; mozzarella
chicken
    sherried chicken & bacon toasts 65
    smoked chicken & ham focaccia 57
chillies
    crab cake toasts 70
    grilled feta cheese with chilli on ciabatta toast 50
    mozzarella-grilled panini with chilli-spiked
        prawns & olives 34

chocolate: double chocolate mango brioche 92
chorizo
    Basque scrambled eggs 42
    chorizo & fennel crostini 37
ciabatta
    brunch bruschetta 41
    grilled feta cheese with chilli on ciabatta toast 50
    Italian steak heroes 87
    roast pepper ciabatta with chopped eggs & olives 58
    salmon & watercress ciabatta 76
    turkey ciabatta with walnuts 69
    Tuscan beans on ciabatta toast with fresh herbs 73
courgettes: smoked chicken & ham focaccia 57
crab cake toasts 70
croissants: ham & cheese croissant 18
croque monsieur 25
cucumber
    Greek salad crostini 62
    minted summer brie on pitta 30

eggs
    Basque scrambled eggs 42
    chive scrambled eggs with brioche 26
    croque monsieur 25
    French toast with maple syrup 21
    glazed beetroot & egg sourdough toasties 84
    ham & cheese croissant 18
    roast pepper ciabatta with chopped eggs & olives 58
    spiced French toast with seasonal berries 95
    toasted cheese sandwich with egg 14
    toasted English muffins with honey-glazed
        bacon & eggs 22

fennel: chorizo & fennel crostini 37
feta cheese
    Greek salad crostini 62
    grilled feta cheese with chilli on ciabatta toast 50
focaccia
    focaccia with roasted cherry tomatoes, basil &
        crispy pancetta 91
    smoked chicken & ham focaccia 57
    toasted aubergine & anchovy focaccia with
        goat's cheese 79
French toast
    French toast with maple syrup 21
    spiced French toast with seasonal berries 95

grapefruit: chorizo & fennel crostini 37
grapes: creamy pan-glazed pork with grapes on
    walnut toasts 80

ham
    croque monsieur 25
    focaccia with roasted cherry tomatoes, basil &
        crispy pancetta 91
    ham & cheese croissant 18
    pear & Roquefort open-face sandwiches 88
    perfect grilled cheese sandwich 54
    smoked chicken & ham focaccia 57
    toasted cheese sandwich with egg 14

ice cream: double chocolate mango brioche 92

leeks: bagels with leeks & cheese 45

mangoes: double chocolate mango brioche 92
maple syrup
    French toast with maple syrup 21
    toasted English muffins with blueberries & bacon 17
mozzarella
    cheese & sun-dried tomato toasts 46
    Italian steak heroes 87
    mozzarella-grilled panini with chilli-spiked prawns &
        olives 34

muffins
    toasted English muffins with blueberries & bacon 17
    toasted English muffins with honey-glazed bacon & eggs 22
mushrooms
    Italian steak heroes 87
    mushroom bruschetta 49
    sausage & mushroom brioche 38
olives
    Greek salad crostini 62
    mozzarella-grilled panini with chilli-spiked prawns &
        olives 34
    roast pepper ciabatta with chopped eggs & olives 58

panini
    mozzarella-grilled panini with chilli-spiked prawns &
        olives 34
    salami, pepper & pine nut panini 33
pear & Roquefort open-face sandwiches 88
peppers
    Basque scrambled eggs 42
    Italian steak heroes 87
    roast pepper ciabatta with chopped eggs & olives 58
    salami, pepper & pine nut panini 33
pitta breads: minted summer brie on pitta 30
pork: creamy pan-glazed pork with grapes on walnut toasts 80
prawns
    avocado prawn toasts 83
    mozzarella-grilled panini with chilli-spiked prawns &
        olives 34

rye toast with roast beef & coleslaw 66

salad leaves
    Greek salad crostini 62
    grilled feta cheese with chilli on ciabatta toast 50
    salami, pepper & pine nut panini 33
    sausage & mushroom brioche 38
salami, pepper & pine nut panini 33
salmon
    hot smoked salmon, tomato & cream cheese bagel 13
    salmon & watercress ciabatta 76
sausage
    sausage & mushroom brioche 38
    see also chorizo; salami
sherried chicken & bacon toasts 65
sourdough bread: glazed beetroot & egg sourdough toasties 84
sweetcorn: toasted English muffins with honey-glazed
    bacon & eggs 22

toast, perfect 10
tomatoes
    Basque scrambled eggs 42
    brunch bruschetta 41
    cheese & sun-dried tomato toasts 46
    focaccia with roasted cherry tomatoes, basil & crispy
        pancetta 91
    Greek salad crostini 62
    hot smoked salmon, tomato & cream cheese bagel 13
    minted summer brie on pitta 30
    perfect grilled cheese sandwich 54
    tempting tomato bruschetta 61
    toasted aubergine & anchovy focaccia with goat's cheese 79
    toasted cheese sandwich with egg 14
    toasted English muffins with honey-glazed bacon & eggs 22
turkey ciabatta with walnuts 69

walnuts, walnut bread
    creamy pan-glazed pork with grapes on walnut toasts 80
    pear & Roquefort open-face sandwiches 88
    turkey ciabatta with walnuts 69
watercress: salmon & watercress ciabatta 76